DAILY INFUSIONS

Books by Gary Hewins

Daily Infusions Series
(devotional series)

Book 1: *Discovering Your Fullness in Christ*
Book 2: *Behold!*
Book 3: *About the Father's Business*

Other Titles

Truth Serum: America's Ever-Increasing Need for Pulpiteers (2017)

DAILY INFUSIONS

Behold!

Dr. Gary Hewins

Daily Infusions
Book 2

Daily Infusions: Behold!
Dr. Gary Hewins

Publisher: Lifepoints at Five Apple Farm
www.Lifepoints.life

ISBN-13: 979-8-218-97122-9

in·fu·sion in-ˈfyü-zhən

Transfusions, by definition, introduce a like element (e.g. blood) into a system to simply increase that element's volume and pressure to achieve a required physiological norm.

Infusions, by definition, introduce an entirely different element into a system to alter its level of vitality and purpose, often with redemptive, restorative, and therapeutic results.

Infuse water with your favorite tea leaves and simply wait as it steeps to alter your afternoon experience of restoration and reflection.

Infuse your bank account with capital and satisfy financial obligations, consider an exotic vacation, and explore the joys of generosity.

Infuse your body, soul, and spirit with the following "infusions" of truth and enjoy an increased volume of the Spirit, an ever-growing appetite for Christ, and invigorating moments of restoration and readiness. The following daily "treatments" will alter your level of spiritual vitality as you discover your fullness in Christ. These are not long-shot experimental treatments but tried-and-true daily infusions based on the immovable promises of God, which are "yes" and "amen" in Christ.

Seek the LORD and his strength; seek his presence continually!
1 Chronicles 16:11 (ESV)

Pastor Gary

Table of Contents

Introduction

In this life, we often become like that which we often behold.

All people behold something. We set our eyes on, pay attention to, study, and eventually offer allegiance to something or someone. We gravitate toward the worship of what we frequently behold. And if we're not careful, we can—and do—become beholden to the object of our worship.

Behold Christ. Live a life not unlike His. Worship Him and Him alone, and remain grateful for what He has done for you.

Be still. Just be. Hold on to Him. Behold!

Behold the Lamb of God, which taketh away the sin of the world.
John 1:29 (KJV)

DAY 1
Behold!

"Be still, and know that I am God;
I will be exalted among the nations,
I will be exalted in the earth."
Psalm 46:10 (ESV)

Be. Infusions, medicinal or spiritual, are best received when one is simply still. Said another way, just "be."

Most everything in this cultural moment screams at us to *do*. Instead, let's *be* for a few minutes. To live a sound and balanced life, a human being cannot always be a "human doing." Simply be. Be still. Be still and know that He is God. Be aware that in this moment, there is no multitasking. Unmask before your Christ and, with Him, be who you truly are. Nestle yourself into the simplicity of being still before the One who has an abiding interest in the real you.

In the many moments and days ahead, you will be infused with encouragement, love, understanding, wisdom, and hope when you settle yourself into the soon-to-be-developed bliss of stillness. In that stillness, you will be enveloped by your newly discovered friend, Silence. Silence will help you be yourself and receive for yourself as you grow into your new self.

Infusibility will necessitate stillness—not idleness. Your stillness will activate your ability to center on the Christ you always knew existed but who remained fogged in by a sea of superfluous distractions and meaningless religiosity. You are about to stop counting your attempts to connect with your Lord.

1

You are about to start encountering Him as He attempts to simply be with you…and in you.

Hold. "God is Spirit, and those who worship Him must worship in spirit and truth" (John 4:24). How does one hold on to the Spirit? In your stillness, hold on! Hold on to the idea that He is holdable and you are moldable. Hold on to the horns of the altar and wait upon your Lord. Be still and hold on with trust, trust that He is caring for you and nurturing you with truth and with His presence. Hold on to a mustard seed of faith to believe that He is advocating on your behalf. Hold on. Seize your "seizable" God; secure His magnificent blessings. Pursue your Lord in the power of the Spirit and diligently seek Him while He may be found. Hold on and be willing to be held yourself. Be still and be held.

Behold.

Fix your inner eyes on Him. Gaze upon Him. At the expense of everything and everyone that attempts to rob you of time with Him, behold His glory. Behold Him first; care for others second. Study His splendor. Reflect on His nobleness. Behold the multifaceted beauty and diversity of the God who demonstrated His love for you. In stillness that is shrouded in many decibels of silence, truly behold Him as the Lamb of God, your Hiding Place, your Defender, your Glory, and the Lifter of your head.

Beholden. Who are we that He is mindful of us? Express to Him the gratitude you have for even having access to His fellowship. We are beholden to Him and Him alone! Be beholden to freely worship Him. Let no debt remain outstanding to another except for love while you earnestly recognize that you owe Christ your adoration, your affection, and your whole heart.

The infusions in the days ahead will be best received in a posture of stillness. Some days you will sit, while other days you will kneel. Occasionally you will seek His face while remaining on yours. The deep awe of Christ that you long for patiently awaits you, just beyond any far-too-casual rhetoric. It will intensify and, as it does, it will refreshingly astonish you. Your Lord will speak to you personally in a safe setting steeped in truth. Be infused with truth. Hold on to His promises. Behold His glory. Remain beholden to Him for all eternity.

Jesus Christ is Lord. Behold the Lamb of God, which taketh away the sin of the world.

———————————

Oh, tend to me today, Lord. I desire stillness, that I may know You even more. Help me to just "be." I want to hold on to You. I long for an infusion of You that will alter me. I seek to behold Your glory. You are the glory and the Lifter of my head. Amen.

DAY 2
Behold the Awe

When he opened the seventh seal,
there was silence in heaven for about half an hour.
Revelation 8:1

"There was silence in heaven for about half an hour."

Not even crickets. The seventh seal, when opened, reveals devastating events, the response to which can only be a holy hush. In the throne room of heaven, people from every nation, tribe, and language will see a grotesque revelation of systematically destructive apocalyptic events that warrant only a well-sustained silence. Even as these events provoke a sustained silence, the One worthy of initiating them will provoke only a sustained awe.

Only One is worthy to open the seal. Only One is sufficiently athoritative to commence such tribulation. He is worthy of eternal tribute because of His demonstrative love and compassion. Consequently, He can exact tribulation upon those still remaining selfishly defiant to His grace.

Yet out of His grace—not out of punitive retribution—He affords the most desperately defiant and deceived another opportunity for redemption by stoking the flames of tribulation. Even then, a loving Christ will pursue those who still desperately oppose Him because He has an even greater desperation to redeem them.

The longing Christ has to purchase the freedom of those most debased at the end of this age warrants a deep silence. He does tread the winepress of the fury of the wrath of God Almighty, but up until the time when there is no longer time for repentance, His fury is for the salvation of souls.

You, unlike many others, are acquiring a taste not just for righteousness, but for the awe of

the Lord. In Christ, you long to experience the awe of God. You understand that knowing your Lord and possessing a deep, reverent awe of Him are synonymous. You understand that an absence of awe is the absence of the ability to behold His splendor. A lack of awe dilutes the intensity of your worship.

Behold Christ, and awe follows. Behold casually, and serve a casual and, at times, unnecessary Lord. You feed on awe, for it separates your Lord from all others that set themselves up against the knowledge of Him. You know deep in your spiritual marrow that reverential awe of the Lord is a natural prerequisite to supernatural moves of His hand.

Any awe of your Lord that has faded is beginning to simmer again, bubbling into a new, reverential brilliance within you. You stand in awe of Him as you behold the clear-as-crystal hues of the jasper, carnelian, and emerald around Him. Flashes of lighting and peals of thunder, once seeming ominous in your youth, are now but sparklers compared to the awe you have of Him who sits on the throne. He sits because "it is finished." His Lordship in your life is now a real, established spiritual protocol for life in the power of the Spirit.

You want awe, for you want deep reverence. You want deep reverence because you want the fullness of the fear of the Lord. You want to walk in the healthy fear of the Lord because it is the beginning of all wisdom. You want awe, and your desire for it is, appropriately, not casual.

An awe of the Lord leads you to wisdom, wisdom to tell others of the awe-inspiring God who died for you. This awe precipitates

6

an awesome silence…and in that silence, you will be as fully alive and spiritually sensitive as you have ever been.

In Christ, you now know to be still—not for stillness' sake, but to cultivate a reverent atmosphere of respect. In your stillness, just be who you truly are, for that is who He died for. In an otherwise desensitized and distracted world, grasp tightly to the resurrection of an awe of The One who *is* resurrection. In that place, behold Him…and see the Holy Spirit move in power.

———————————

As undeserving as I am, by Your grace, would You help me truly stand in awe of You? Share with me, if You will, Your supremacy that transcends words. Take me to a rock higher than I and to a deeper understanding of true reverence for You. Amen.

DAY 3
Behold The Anointed One

But you have an anointing from the Holy One,
and all of you know the truth.
1 John 2:20

Jesus is the Messiah, The Anointed One. Behold The Select, Empowered One. He is empowered by the Spirit to preach the gospel. He was sent our way to heal the brokenhearted and to proclaim liberty for the captives. He was anointed to provide recovery of sight to the blind and to set the oppressed free.

Christ is both a proclaimer and a provider. That which He proclaims, He provides in Himself, in the same way the oil of the Spirit was rubbed and worked into Him to create Oneness between them.

Behold! The heavens opened to The Anointed One. He saw the Spirit of God descending like a dove and alighting upon Him. The Nazarene, prophetically born in Bethlehem, grew in wisdom and stature and, at the appointed time, was anointed. Christ was clearly appointed and anointed to fulfill righteousness and set the captives free.

In Christ, you too are anointed. You have an anointing from the Holy One. You know the truth, and you know it is the truth that sets people with bludgeoned, aching souls free. You are empowered by the same Spirit that descended upon and empowered Christ. You have been "doved."

The Spirit of the Sovereign Lord flows through your compassion and spiritual gifts to the brokenhearted and captive people in your sphere of influence. In Christ, you eagerly desire spiritual gifts. Through them, the anointing of the Holy One enables you to do even greater works than Christ. How, apart from the anointing, could anyone even consider doing works of eternal value? The thought of doing greater works than Christ apart from the anointing of the Spirit in life and ministry is sheer absurdity.

The anointing of Christ has been rubbed and worked into you. You have the capacity to believe for and see come to pass things which, apart from the Spirit, you need not even consider. With Christ, all things are possible! Christ is the Anointed One. You have an anointing from the Holy One; therefore, you are equipped by the Spirit to live with the resolute belief that all things are possible.

You are anointed. You have an anointing. Heaven opened and shared with you the Spirit of the Father and the Spirit of the Son. Like Christ, you are a proclaimer. You proclaim good news, you provide wisdom, and you speak truth. Through your earnest and humble proclamations, the Spirit convicts, instructs, rebukes, restores, and makes whole those who are fractured.

The Spirit of the Sovereign Lord is upon Jesus. Your Sovereign God has anointed Him. What Jesus has, He shares. Christ has shared with you the anointing that breaks the yoke of oppression. Live in the confidence of the anointing of the Spirit. Speak, teach, and counsel, knowing you are anointed for His service. Maximize your personal awareness of that power. Be humbled by the privilege to wield it. Eagerly desire spiritual gifts

10

that release the anointing, and grow ever more humble in the process.

Deflect any personal credit you may receive as you gratefully enjoy the results of the anointing. If you are undeservingly the recipient of vain flattery, stand behind Christ, your Hiding Place. Reverently pursue the sweet fragrance of His anointing, but desire no power from His empowerment.

Yes, you have an anointing from the Holy One, but it is given only to serve the alienated, the unwanted, the confused, the traumatized, the lost, and the hopeless.

Be faithful in a few things, and God will give you charge over many things. Whichever of the "many things" you find yourself involved with, walk humbly with your God. Lay hands on others, as though laying His hands on them. See others, as though seeing through His eyes. Impart to others what is truly His. Be present with them under the anointing of the Holy One and enjoy the bewildering privilege of ministering to "the least of these" under the anointing of the Spirit of God. Remember that as you do so, you are also doing it unto Him.

May the lighting of the "Dove" be the source by Whom you minister to those around you. As you do so, always bear in mind that you are also ministering to your Lord, who will continue to light upon you time and time again. What a tragedy it would be to live as though you have no anointing. Behold! You have an anointing from The Anointed One.

———————

Apart from You, I can do nothing. Greater are You that is in me than he that is in the world. Light upon me like a dove and anoint me for Your service today. I pray for a yoke-breaking anointing that liberates the captives I meet today. Constrain me by Your love. Amen.

DAY 4
Behold Your Hiding Place

You are my hiding place;
You shall preserve me from trouble;
You shall surround me with songs of deliverance. Selah
Psalm 32:7 (NKJV)

Adam, the first man, was never more like a boy than right after he first sinned. Flooded with the awkwardness of first-time toxic feelings like guilt, shame, and remorse, he did what comes naturally to any overwhelmed little boy: he hid. He hid in the trees. In this fallen and fractured world, our instinctive first move after sinning is to hide. Adam hid privately in the trees, unlike Christ, who publicly hung on one. Adam attempted to cover his shame; the second Adam, Christ, scorned it.

In a fallen world, hurting people look for places to hide. People hide behind their personal masks, their well-rehearsed denials, their adamant rationalizations, even their best-fabricated, well-woven deceptions.

In the kingdom of God, believers also look for a place to hide...but our hiding place is unique. If we play Twenty Questions and start with the initial inquiry: "Is this a person, place, or thing?" we find the answer a bit mystifying. Our hiding

14

place, Christ Himself, is both a person and a place. How does this work?

God is omnipresent—He is everywhere at the same time. Yet His presence can be manifested in such a way that you are aware of His presence with greater sensitivity and awe. This awareness makes the person also a place…your Hiding Place. His presence is a sure experiential reality to those who seek Him in this time and space.

The weightiness of His glory lifts from you the burdens you carry. Hidden in Him, that

weightiness is your glory and the lifter of your head. You are a hider of the highest caliber, for you hide in Christ, who is the highest standard. You hide *in* Him; you do not hide *from* Him. This reality fosters in you an ability to confront and deal with a world that delights in exposing your every flaw.

Your preservation and safety is found in Christ. In Him you hide. He envelops you in times of doubt and despair. He is your Shield. As His follower, Christ stands before you while you draft behind Him. He is your Hiding Place.

In Him, you preserve your integrity, you tell the truth, you take full personal responsibility, you blame no other. That's what you do, for you follow the One who blamed no other, even as He took on the responsibility for the sins of others. In Him you hide.

In your hiding, you remain hedged in, protected, and buffeted. You are strangely surrounded by and shrouded in divine musical soundings. You are hidden in Christ amid glorious harmonies of soprano, alto, tenor, and bass tones. In your restful hiding, you are sustained by songs of deliverance. In Him you hide; thus, in Him you rest and enjoy the inevitable liberty to come.

People hide from one another, from the callings on their lives, and from the responsibilities inherently associated with their callings. Not you. In Christ, you march in lockstep with Him. His pace is your pace. His direction is your direction. Where He goes, you go, for you are in Him and He is in you. You are clothed in His compassion, and you are cloaked in His priestly authority. When manipulative flattery comes your way, you are hidden in Christ. Amid mockery and ridicule, you are hidden in Christ. When temptation seeks to move you, you remain hidden in Christ.

Behold your Hiding Place. Your Hiding Place is as formidable now as He has ever been. You are hidden in Him. Your spiritual walk is glazed with intimacy. Like a rabbi slowly slipping his prayer shawl over his head, you are hidden in and closely, personally connected with Christ in the your own private Holy of Holies. He is your Panic Room, your Prayer Closet, and your Safe Childhood Clubhouse.

He is your Comfortable Place, the One with whom you can be completely and safely vulnerable.

———————————

Envelop me, my Lord. Shroud me in Your glory. Hide me in You, if but for a moment. Douse me in a fountain of hope, that I be readied to refresh, renew, and revive those You lead me to love. Amen.

DAY 5
Behold Your Lead Singer

"The Lord your God is with you, the Mighty Warrior who saves. He will take great delight in you; in his love he will no longer rebuke you, but will rejoice over you with singing."
Zephaniah 3:17

In Christ, your Hiding Place, there is singing. In God's presence is fullness of joy, and joy is often accompanied by song. In His manifest presence, there are sounds, notes, melodies, and rhythmic themes that unite in harmony to create anointed songs with anointed lyrics sung by an Anointed Lead Singer. Christ rejoices and sings over you. Who could better render songs of deliverance than Christ Himself? Your Mighty Warrior sings over you.

What does He sing? Your Hiding Place sings truth. Truth Himself sings truth over you and, in so doing, His truth sets you free. He sings melodies of deliverance to the captives. The beauty of His vocals facilitate emancipation. Liberty flows from His mouth. His melodious voice sets you free from sin and selfishness. His lips release living lyrics of liberation. He is the Leader of the Band, and the band plays and sings for you, over you. You are wrapped in songs of deliverance that comfort you like a warm blanket.

Above you even now, a song is being sung. Tunes are broadcast from on high, but not in the voices of heavenly beings or cherubs or seraphim. No, your Lord Himself has broken out in song over your brokenness and confusion. He takes great delight in you, and He rejoices over you with singing. What are you that He is mindful of you? You are His, and Your God serenades you.

You sing, too, because He first sang over you. You sing psalms, hymns, and spiritual songs to God, making music to Him with gratitude in your heart. You, a bruised reed, have been repaired and have thus become an instrument of worship. You sing to Him a new song as you seek to express your ever-increasing appreciation for Him.

Beneath the balcony of heaven, you may at times feel a foreboding chill, a sense of being alone, overwhelmed, and overshadowed. If so, listen closely for the approaching sounds of heavenly music. Listen attentively to the lyrics of deliverance. Rise up when you sense such singing. It is your Lord! Rise up and greet Him with a song of your own. Your life is a musical, so sing and make melody in your heart to God today.

When life in this frail, fallen world insists on a dirge, fight back with songs of praise! You have breath; therefore, you know to praise Him, exalt Him, magnify Him—first for who He is, and subsequently for who He will soon be. You march to the beat of a different drummer. You are a worshiper of the One True God.

When you feel isolated and confused and far from God, He, wanting you clear-minded and close to Him, conducts His own orchestra and sings to you. Symphonic deliverance takes place as the warmth of His breath defrosts your heart. You worship a God who sings and makes melody over you just when you need it most. His voice beckons, woos you even, a beautiful, rhythmically perfect tune calling for your swift return. He will never leave you nor forsake you, even as you limp about in a daze. No, as He breaks out in song, He breaks your shackles.

Listen closely for the approaching sounds of His beautiful voice, and arise when you sense Him drawing near. It is your Lord! Greet Him with joy, and then be still before Him. Behold Him. Be beholden to Him in worship, and enjoy His presence.

He is even now singing over you.

May I be as free as needed to minster Your grace today. Sing over me like a mother would over a crying baby. Sing over me lyrics of liberation. I love You so, O Lord. Sing over me. Even a whisper will do. Amen.

DAY 6
Behold His Unhurried Ways

Wait for the Lord;
be strong and take heart
and wait for the Lord.
Psalm 27:14

    This world is often harried and hurried. Today's man-centered system pushes us to only begrudgingly wait for anything…and "anything" almost always takes too long. A brief instant is now the only tolerable delay. The world wants for much, yet it wants nothing to do with waiting.

    Speed has, in no small manner, helped the world form its identity. Wanting more and more in faster and faster increments has become the acceptable hallmark of today's civilization. The "hares" of this world have been deemed obsolete, as only the "tortoises" are now tolerable.

    Lurking nearby you is a masked villain with a rap sheet as long as his arm. He wants to steal your joy. His name is Urgency, and he is a tyrant. His mission is to create emergencies and crises in your world and then drive you to impulsive reactions. He wants you to grow too fast, to be quick to react, to be slow to reflect. He thrusts you toward measuring quantity, while he compels you to sprint past quality. He loves the wasteful impulse purchase. He is quickly pursuing you, for he loves compelling you to move at a heightened pace in order to render you even more vulnerable.

You are truly resisting the hurried pattern of this world that offers only distraction, flightiness, and the power of the rush. This firmly established culture desperately wants you to conform to a life of rapidity. You are no stranger to this scheme. You are aware of the hurriedness of the world.

But although you oppose this mindset, have you not projected this very same pattern onto

your Lord? Do you not expect Him to conform to your well-adopted, man-made timelines? Does your current thinking not have a conditioned and conditional pace? You expect things, even from God, on your own vaguely defined schedule, a timetable established and greatly influenced by the world you live in. Have you unknowingly put your own chronological expectations on the Divine?

Is He not the same yesterday, today, and forever? Have you not held Him to a far shorter timeline than His eternal essence defines? Has He not always operated in an unhurried fashion?

Your Hiding Place is Christ. He is a Person. He is also a Place where His Presence can be palpable. When you allow yourself to simply "be"—when you wait, when you still yourself, when you worship and operate on God's timeline, when you truly behold Him—your friendship deepens.

Your new middle name is "Linger." You know to linger in the presence and glory of your Lord. When you linger with Him, He will share more with you. He will give you greater insight. He has more to impart to you when you linger. You are a lingerer, hidden in Christ and listening to His songs of deliverance. You, in Christ, are a hidden, liberated lingerer who beholds your King, who waits before Him, and who is beholden to the Ancient of Days.

In Christ, the only times you hurry are when you race to seize the power of patience and when you run boldly and confidently to the throne of grace. Patience, though nearly extinct, is skilled at waiting for you to introduce yourself and then become its lifelong friend. Patience waits for you to want to wait, with contentment, on your Lord.

In Christ, you are patient. You wait on your unhurried Lord. When not running in the flesh, you walk in the Spirit, unhurriedly enjoying and even grazing on forbearance and long-suffering. You are finding a lower gear with more powerful torque that is seasoning your life with greater joy and effectiveness.

Christ is your rest. He makes you lie down in green pastures. Wait for the Lord; be strong, and let your heart take courage; wait for the Lord! Your unhurried Lord is worth any wait. But do not wait in idleness. Wait on Him actively, hopefully, dynamically. Wait in prayer for Him as you walk out His calling for your life.

Soak. Linger. Behold His unhurried ways.

———————————

I cherish a walk with You. Why, in my zeal, do I so often see You in my rearview mirror? Forgive my jog. Have patience when I sprint. Amble with me today, and I with You. Tend to me today as we walk together. Amen.

DAY 7
Behold the Manger

So they hurried off and found Mary and Joseph,
and the baby, who was lying in the manger.
Luke 2:16

A manager manages. Managers are important figures, both in industry and in life. They develop alluring brands and monetize intriguing products.

Innkeepers are managers; they manage people, vacancy rates, pricing, and quality control. Inn managers determine levels of hospitality and frequency of visits. They make decisions as to who may reserve space and who may not. Thus, inn capacity is a managed resource.

When it comes to Christ, you are no manager. You are a manger. A manger is a simple feeding trough. You graze on daily spiritual bread, and then people feed from you. You feed others well. You are a manger, constantly being emptied and filled back up again. You are always open, and you're always hospitable. As a manger, you understand the pricelessness of the indwelling Christ. You understand the messiness of ministry and the need to feed both those with nowhere to lay their heads and kings who come bearing gifts. Yes, you will forever remain a manger. You are sovereignly chosen to be a restful and hospitable dwelling for the Spirit of Christ, the Son of the Most High God.

26

Christ feels at home in you. You have the capacity and longing to be continually emptied of your old self and filled with the Spirit of God. You will not manage your Lord, but you will allow Him to manage you. You are now and will forever be a manger, a comfortable dwelling place of the One True God. Through you, His manger, He feels welcome to cry out to a lost and dying world. The old you passed away long ago. Now you hold new life, new hope, and new possibilities.

Many seem to know there is a God, but He seems to them far away. You have far greater understanding. You worship Emmanuel, "God with us." You know He is always with you; He dwells in you, His manger—"Christ in you, the hope of glory." He lounges in the weightiness of your worship. Your worship is His "food" many know nothing about.

Some people live as though Christ is near them. At times, they manage Him; at other times, they lack room or capacity for Him, sometimes, they even "monetize" a conditional friendship with Him.

You, however, remain a manger. You exist for Him to fill and occupy you, both in the most critical and helpless of situations as well as in the most worshipful of contexts.

God has taken on flesh and made His dwelling among us. You have seen His glory, the glory of the one and only Son, full of grace and truth. He is full; therefore, as His manger, you are full. He is full of grace; thus, as His manger, you are full of grace. He is full of truth; consequently, as His manger, you are full of truth. You have within you the mind of Christ, the authority of Christ, the word of Christ, and the love of Christ.

Manage not. Just be. Be that manger. Hold Him, cradle Him like you would a precious baby. Behold Him and see how beautiful He is. Be beholden to Him and carry Him to others suffering from a gospel famine. You are a walking, talking feeding trough inhabited by Christ Himself, the Bread of Life.

You are interacting with people starving for attention, worth, and love, people whose palates long for something with taste and texture to fill and satisfy them. The world manages them. You feed them.

Managers schedule, scrutinize, and evaluate from a distance. You remain near the epicenter of all Christ does because, as His manger, you are centered in His will.

———————————

I am Your prophetic manger. I feed others. I exist for the Holy Spirit to be cradled and at rest in my heart and mind. Should I attempt to manage You, correct me. Should I withhold from others, instruct me. May there remain no context in which I lack the humility to serve You. Amen.

DAY 8
Behold The Lamb

The next day John saw Jesus coming toward him, and said,
"Behold! The Lamb of God
who takes away the sin of the world!"
John 1:29 (ESV)

Most anyone in the Galilee could make a quick and common identification of Jesus of Nazareth. Yet Jesus of Nazareth was neither common nor fully, accurately, or truly identified. Jesus is like a brilliant diamond held up before a lamp and slowly turned. Each facet of the stone reflects a different ray of His divine nature. Each aspect of His nature can easily cut through any barrier to freedom in our lives.

Historians identified Jesus. His enemies identified Him. His own hometown folk could easily identify Him. But they did not all truly behold Him. To exhaustively behold and appreciate the Christ may require all eternity. At various points within His three-year ministry, even those closest to Him barely began to build upon their original recognition of the Nazarene. They eventually made progress in their comprehension of His true identity—even at the cost of their lives. We have seen His glory, they said, the glory of the one and only Son, who came from the Father, full of grace and truth.

You too are a beholder. You are now adding to your portfolio of experiential understanding of the Nazarene. Using His living

Word, you are beholding His beauty, although you have never seen Him face to face. In fact, your increasing intimacy with your Lord provides a more accurate identification of Christ than that of those who laid eyes on Him from only yards away. You are seeing Him with ever-increasing clarity. You are "beholding." You are developing into an aficionado of beholding. You are making beholding an art form because you are willing to be still and hold Him. You have eyes to see and ears to hear what the Spirit of God is saying to you about Him.

Many saw only a man. You see the Lord. Many only see a teacher; you behold a Wise Confidant. Others see a master; you behold a Friend to serve. Many see an elusive and distant God; you run boldly to the throne of grace. Many see a cultural revolutionary; you see a personal Revolutionary. You live and move and have your being at an alternative level, speaking, listening, loving, and worshiping a truly behold-able, personal Lord. Your beholding is aided by another, who is to be beheld in His own right: the Spirit of the Living God. He reveals, quickens, reveals, and informs as you mature as a beholder.

Many quickly identify the risen Christ as one who simply sits at the right hand of the Father, entertaining prayers of supplication. The masses want for a King who simply takes song requests on a paper napkin. Most see God only as a generous giver, filling orders when called upon to do so. You have *beheld* the Giver. Yet you are growing beyond such limited, juvenile definitions of His essence.

You celebrate your Lord as a taker! You are now beholding the Greatest of Takers. While many shower Him with requests, you thank Him for what He has taken. Behold, He has taken you out of the darkness only to place you in His marvelous light. He has taken you from toxic relationships that could have hurt you. He has absorbed and taken away your guilt. He has scorned your shame. He has relieved you of sorrows, the sorrows once embedded in His own being.

You behold the perplexingly docile Lamb in all His innocence, and you behold a straightforward, necessary Taker. Behold the Lamb that taketh, that taketh, that taketh away the sin of the world. Where your sin abounds, His grace does much more abound. He takes and takes and takes from you as He takes and takes and takes you closer to your completion in Christ Jesus. He carries you unto completion, taking from you along the way to lighten your load and make you gentle and humble of heart.

I wish to gaze and remain affixed upon the beauty and innocence of Your Holiness, Lord. I behold and focus on Your divine power, Your "dunamis" that is found in meekness. Your potency remains at work in the weakest of vessels, and for this, I thank You. I behold You, my Lamb, today. Amen.

DAY 9
Behold The Way

Jesus answered, "I am the way and the truth and the life.
No one comes to the Father except through me."
John 14:6

This world has not yet embraced Him who is "The Way." Christ is The Way; hence, to be without Christ is to be wayward. Our world is accustomed to trending in one direction, only to quickly divert and trend in another. The world is wayward and rapidly spiraling down toward greater self-sufficiency and self-glorification. Idolatry and the love of money is on the rise, and evil is taking stronger root. The world is looking for a way while missing The Way.

In Christ, you are neither wayward nor moving downward. You are focused and looking and living upward. Your words are uplifting and your actions upright. Christ is The Way, and Christ is your way. He assures you of success as you follow His lead.

Your life in Christ is not predictable. He is not static but dynamic, challenging, and instructive. He is forever the same, yet He is ever-changing in the ways in which He shows you varying facets of His love. You are moving onward toward new experiences in Christ. In your life, Christ is trending strong. He is entrusting you with opportunities to grow, expand, and enhance your life in Him. Your life in Him is an adventure. He came that you may have life, and life more abundantly. You are moving onward into greater responsibilities. To you, much has been given, and from you, much will be required.

In Christ, you not only focus upward in worship, but you also look outward with compassion. You see others as your Lord sees them. You see others through grace. You can and do examine yourself, even while seeing the hearts of others. Some look only at people's outward appearance, but you, like your Lord, look at their hearts. You see things others will not even consider. You are a treasure hunter. You find treasures within people, and you unearth and enjoy them.

In Christ, ministry is not awkward to you. You minister to others in the power of the Spirit and with the grace of Christ. You walked away from and lost touch with "awkward" long ago. You are not intimidated by or ashamed of the gospel. To you, the glorious gospel is the power of God. You will not cower. You have truth within you, and you do not want that truth to remain hidden. You do not withhold from others the very truth that will set them free. You hold the keys to the kingdom, and you walk with an authority and confidence rooted and established in Christ, ready to be shared. He is the way; He is your Way. You willingly confess Him before men and, in turn, He confesses you to His Father.

You are a sojourner, an alien passing through this world, yet you are on a mission. You know your citizenship is in heaven. You are, even now, seated in heavenly realms with every spiritual blessing in Christ. You know where you are headed. Your destiny is heavenward, but your orientation is now evangelistic. You know that night is coming when no one can work, so you labor now. You share The Way with the wayward. You pray over the drunkard. You seize those headed downward. Spiritually speaking, you are outwardly mobile, upwardly mindful, inwardly aware, and fervently onward in your pursuit of the fullest, richest, most authentic life you could ever live as you walk in the love of the One who is The Way. Waiting for you, a light amid darkness, is a reward that reflects your stewardship of this incredible, opportunity-filled life. Zealously move onward today in Christ.

––––––––––––––––––

Lord, I can move today in many directions if You remain my Way. All things work for my good when You are my Way. Show me the way for me to forever see You as my only Way. I love You from every direction. Amen.

DAY 10
Behold The Truth

Jesus answered, "I am the way and the truth and the life.
No one comes to the Father except through me."
John 14:6

Deceit and falsehood are the demented offspring of the father of lies. The accuser of the brethren has been a murderer from the beginning, not holding to the truth, for there is no truth in him. He is a false witness, a perjurer of truth. He will never be a true witness. His lying lips are an abomination to the Lord.

This false witness will not go unpunished. He who breathes out lies will perish. He generates nothing; he has no creativity or original thought, so counterfeiting is His only option. He and his lies will one day be bathed in the lake of fire. He repeats his lies often. He redundantly tells the same lie over and over again, which leads to familiarity, which leads to deception, which leads to the acceptance of lies as truth.

In Christ, you have learned to speak a new language, the language of truth. You can speak the truth in love. You can worship in spirit and in truth. Your truthful lips will endure forever. You know the truth, and you know the truth will set you free. You wear the fashionable belt of truth. You are sanctified by the truth; His word is truth. You call on the name of the Lord in truth. You bear no false witness against your neighbor; in fact, you love your neighbor enough to share the truth. You have the maturity to receive and handle truthful and constructive criticism. You possess and are possessed by an ample degree of humility.

In Christ, you are saturated in truth. You are accustomed to truth. You boldly proclaim the truth. Truth is your "new normal." You know how to rightly divide the word of truth. You read truth, pray truth, and meditate upon truth day and night.

Your integrity is based on truth, and your integrity is protected by its bodyguard, conviction. Your very heart, where truth is hidden, becomes convicted at the mere thought of sharing a half-truth. Your truth is highly protected by the Spirit of the Living God so that you might not sin against Him. You are so touched by truth that you quickly discern half-truths as easily as you do full-on lies. A gift of discernment is available to and often employed by you.

In Christ, you walk in truth. You talk in truth, liberating those who limp in deception and mumbling confusion. To you, truth is your life. Christ is the Truth. Christ is your life. You are a blood-bought, born-again eyewitness to the power and presence of the Spirit of God Himself. You have not placed your hand on a Bible, for the Bible is written on the tablet of your heart. You have not sworn an oath; you have entered into the New Covenant. You are a credible witness, a living epistle read by all around you.

Proclaim the truth from the rooftops! Personify truth in the marketplace. Walk in truth; run in truth. Saturate yourself in truth. Love others with the genuine truth of a loving God who truthfully loves you and has demonstrated that love by dying for you and the whole world, that all may know and be set free by the truth.

The world seeks to brainwash you with lies. God's Word washes your brain and enables you to operate with the mind of Christ. You do not fall prey to propaganda or emotional appeals that seek to tear you away from your Lord, the embodiment of truth. Behold the truth!

You are undeniable Truth, my King. You are my Emancipator. Who else can set and keep me free? Keep me honest with You. Please preserve the sacredness of our friendship. I so need You. I trust You. Amen.

DAY 11
Behold The Life

Jesus answered, "I am the way and the truth and the life.
No one comes to the Father except through me."
John 14:6

With but a handful of the dust of the ground, God's breath became a living being. Breath begat breath. From dust, Adam was quickened. Adam was a living, functioning organism, and within him was life that originated and emanated from God Himself. From dust came man, and imparted to man was life. Adam was created by the Father in the image of God the Son and God the Holy Spirit.

In Christ, you relish the reality that you too are alive and functioning. You celebrate life and breath and the nearness of the One who created you, embroidering you in your mother's womb. You are alive; should that not be enough? There is so much more born of God's divine extravagance. The Giver of life is also the Giver of abundant life. The *zōē* life of Christ has been imparted to you. Your biology was the first wave of your life, but then you received the impartation of the vital, genuine, abundant *zōē* life of Christ. You are far more than a physical body.

In Him, you have been gifted with eternal vitality. You went through not the wide gate but the narrow gate. As you did, your Lord, seeing your faith, saw it essential to infuse you with His eternal vitality. You are not only alive; you are alive in Him. Not only are you alive in Him, but He is fully alive in you! You may be perishing physically, but inwardly you are infused with imperishable immortality. Beyond breathing in and breathing out, you are spiritually infused with the absolute fullness of life in Christ. Your breathing will one day be labored, yet He labored that you may eternally enjoy His breath of life. You are animated in His life. You are distinctively consecrated by His life in you. He is your life-giving source of zeal and spiritual vigor. He came that you might have life and that you might have it more abundantly. He means *abundantly*. The abundant life is a great abundance of Christ, the hope of glory, in you.

Do not let this divine life be hindered, hobbled, or hampered in any way by the inferior one, the one who comes to kill, steal, and destroy. Christ's life in you is special, otherworldly, and God-originated. God ordained for you to commune with Him. You have the essence of Christ's life within you even now.

This life in you is illuminating, purposeful, and revelatory. In Him is life, and that life is the light of men. You are a city set upon a hill. The Source of the ever-unveiling life of Christ has made His home in you. Creativity rooted in the life of Christ lives in you. The warmth of His life is enjoyed in you. Christ—and Christ's life in you—is patient, compassionate, sacrificial, and never-ending.

Many fear death. The life of Christ assures you that you will move from life unto life. Others may move from life unto death; you, however, will move from this life to even more life, life eternal. There is no death for you. Perfect love casts out fear. You have no fear of death, for perfect love overcame death, hell, and the grave. You know you are on God's mind and in His heart. You are free to live freely without fear, trepidation, or worry. You are free to live, and to live large. All the documentation exists to certify that you are now and will forever be legally justified by the Righteous Judge. He is the Way and the Truth and the Life within you.

A divine library of one book clearly identifies you as having been born into this new life. It was signed and notarized by the blood of Christ, and it places you in the bloodline of Christ. You are sealed by the Spirit of God, and you will forever remain a dwelling place of the abundant *zōē* life of Christ.

I look to You for life today—not the meaning of life, nor the length of my life, nor the sparing of my life. I look to You today to be my life. I behold You, O Life within me. Amen.

DAY 12
Behold Your Rest

When you lie down, you will not be afraid;
when you lie down, your sleep will be sweet.
Proverbs 3:24

In Christ, you will amble your way into a deep sleep that satisfies and refreshes your body and soul. Your Lord has ordained for you a precious sleep to relish and enjoy. He took Abram into a deep, peaceful, passive, covenantal sleep, and you—like Abram—will also receive His gift of deep sleep. When you lie down, you will be neither anxious nor afraid. You have nothing to fear. Your sleep is laced with deep, sweet, lingering trust. Your Lord wants you to both sleep and dwell in safety. Your burden is easy and light, but your sleep is heavy.

He is your Shalom, your abiding rest. He is the Giver of sleep to His beloved. He has fullness of rest for you to enjoy. He has created green pastures for your lounging pleasure. He speaks to you in your slumber and sustains you by giving you an intermission from work and concerns. You have great reason in your soul to trust and place your confidence in Him and His ability to bring you rest.

He sleeps through storms, and you can and will do the same. He is Jehovah Rapha, the Lord your Healer. His healing will come upon you like a warm blanket.

As you look away from sleeplessness and toward Him, He brings you perfect peace. You dwell in, lie in, and sleep in His safety. He is the Lord of your night, and He is ever present as you slumber. In your sleep, He ministers to you, even speaking directly to you in your dreams. You are an available, restful follower who is prepared to hear His voice in the still of the night.

You follow your Lord, the One who intimately knows your need for a respite. Christ can anoint you to sleep beyond your own ability or understanding to do so. Your body submits to His command to rest. He who keeps you will neither slumber nor sleep so that you can slumber and sleep in Him.

He will present you with a new dawn to be enjoyed because you have had optimal rest. New possibilities are orchestrated for you to flourish in the days ahead. As you rest in Him, He plans His divine calendar for you. Divine appointments will be abundantly scheduled, for your calendar is His. He plans and prepares you as you sleep. Slowly slide into His guiltless rest. Allow His Word to work in power in you as you sleep. Jehovah Shalom will free you from sleeplessness as your heart desires Him. You are insulated from intrusions that are intended to exhaust and deplete you. By day, you are a vibrant follower of Christ, for your nightly rest is rich.

When you lie down, your sleep will be sweet. In peace you will both lie down and sleep, for the Lord Himself will make you dwell in safety. He speaks to you even in your slumber and protects you as you sleep…even from your own worries. It is in vain that you arise early and go to bed late, eating the bread of anxious toil, for He gives sleep to his beloved. Trust Him to minister rest to you. He is your rest. He remains your fullness.

Many count sheep, but He counts you as one of His flock. He will shepherd you into sorely needed, well-deserved, restful sleep. Your Shepherd knows your need for peace. Do not settle for a peace you can grow to understand, but instead relish the truth that His peace transcends all understanding.

Know this: when you need sleep the most, He can and will make you lie down in green pastures. He will personally lead you beside the still waters. He is your Sabbath. He is your rest. He is your peace that revives, restores, renews, and revitalizes your life.

Speak to me Lord, even as I slumber. Fill my mind and dreams with Your Word, Your presence, Your intentions, and Your future. You are my Sabbath, and I rest in You. Amen.

DAY 13
Behold Your Lifeguard

*The law was brought in so that the trespass might increase.
But where sin increased, grace increased all the more…*
Romans 5:20

The grace of God is expansive, refreshing, and never-ending. In fact, in Christ, you have been submerged in a pool of undeserved grace. You relish its fresh waters. Having first dipped your toe in that inviting reservoir, you now know the beauty and relief found in being saturated by grace. You are gliding through life in a grace provided specifically, personally, for you by Christ, Your Lifeguard.

Where your sin abounds, grace outflanks it and abounds even more. You are baptized and immersed in grace. You can dive into its depths and never touch bottom, because there is no bottom to grace. Today, you get to freestyle in a pool of grace, grace so inviting and irresistible that it makes sin resistible. Relish the irresistibility of God's grace. You have been saved by grace through faith. This is not your own doing; it is the gift of God. It is not the result of works, so that you may not boast. There is a monstrosity of grace overshadowing you, blocking any potential shame from receiving life-giving light. Grace holds such an allure to you that the temptations you once struggled with spark little to no interest anymore.

50

His grace is sufficient for you. His power, even now, is made perfect in your weakness. Go ahead: boast in your weakness; the power of Christ rests upon you. Just when you think grace has run out, He gives more grace.

You not only walk in grace; you walk in humility. You understand that God opposes the proud but gives grace to the humble. You have a divinely ordained daily opportunity to humbly, yet boldly, approach the throne of grace with confidence. You have access to the royal palace each and every moment of every day. You can access the eternal grace of God, grace you recognize is only accessible through the blood of Jesus Christ. Your Messiah, foreknowing your needs, has already lovingly provided all the grace you will ever require…and more. His grace, through His love shed abroad in your heart by the Holy Spirit, is sufficient for you now and for tomorrow and for eternity. You humbly acknowledge that His grace affords you that which you do not deserve.

His grace also miraculously gives you access to mercy. You enjoy the mercy of God through His grace as He mercifully withholds from you now and tomorrow and for all eternity that which you *do* deserve. You have been allocated the grace to enjoy what you could never deserve as well as the freedom to live mercifully apart from the punishment you actually deserve.

You are deeply loved by the one true God who established a way for you when there seemed to be no way. He is the way. The way of grace has been laid out before you.

The abundance of grace that is yours in Christ today can now be extended by you to others. The limitless grace apportioned to you can now be allocated to others while never diminishing your own supply. You are a dispenser of grace because you realize that but for the grace of God, you would go astray. Extend grace just as Christ extended grace to you. What does the Lord require of you? To act justly and to love mercy and to walk humbly with your God. Make it your mission to swim wholeheartedly today in the sea of underserved favor, unfathomable freedom, and God-ordained grace…all for His glory.

You look for opportunities to be gracious and to love the seemingly unlovable. The grace of God provides you with lenses to see as He sees. You see others differently. You have vision others deny. You perceive others through spectacles of grace.

Behold Christ, your Lifeguard. He graciously watches you from His perch, desiring only to see you swim in His grace, and then, to invite others to plunge into that pool by faith.

Lord, forgive me when I consider sin to be casual in light of Your grace. Convict me, Spirit of God. In light of my error, show me the necessity of having a pliable and teachable heart. Keep me sensitive to anything and anyone that seeks to come between us. Amen.

DAY 14
Behold His Grandeur

Lord, our Lord,
how majestic is your name in all the earth!
You have set your glory
in the heavens.
Psalm 8:1

Your Lord is the Son of the Father who is the Giver of every good and perfect gift. Therefore, your Lord is good. He is oh so perfect. Like His Father, He is generous with you. You are called to serve Him, glorify Him, befriend Him, and continually pursue Him. You have access to a divine court that others know not of; many crassly deny its existence. Your Lord is the image of the invisible God. He, like the wind, blows wherever He pleases. Like a cool breeze, He is not seen, but He is near.

Your Lord is the firstborn over all creation. He knows the limitations of your flesh and can sympathize with your weaknesses because, although He is God, He became flesh—He became one of us. He knows pain, fatigue, and sorrow. He knows you, and He knows what it is like to be you. He is your wisdom for solving problems and facing conflict.

He rules over all things. He spoke, and light came into existence. His voice shakes the cedars of Lebanon; His voice rattles, pierces, and yet stills the human heart. His voice reverberates from His throne, and you are its echo.

54

He is your Creator and your ongoing source of creativity. He created all things, both seen and unseen.

He knows all things. His knowledge supersedes the collective knowledge of all other beings. His omniscience encompasses all matters known and unknown by humankind.

He is the Alpha—He is First. He is before all things. He is both the beginning and before

the beginning ever was. He is the First Firstfruit. Before Abraham was, He was the *I AM,* the all-sufficient, self-existing, and all-knowing One.

All that is falling apart is resisting Him, though He holds all things together. As Alpha, He has the first word—in fact, He *is* the Word. As Omega, He has the last word; even then, He is still the Word. He is the ever-present, ever-being, ever-loving, uncreated, never-ceasing-to-be One pursuing your heart with an eternal love wrapped in eternal grace and laced with eternal mercy. His Presence is your present, to be opened and enjoyed daily.

Death was duped into thinking it had lasting power and a victorious finality. Your Lord, your Life, overcame death. The fragrance of your worship overcomes the stench of death. Your Lord is victory. In all things He has supremacy. Fullness dwells in Him, and He remains your undepletable reservoir of satisfaction and meaning. He moves about, reconciling all things and desiring to reconcile all people to Himself, that none should perish.

Your Lord makes peace through His blood shed on a cross. He is your peace even when you are cross. He is your direction at every crossroad. He is the crossbeam that strengthens and renders your faith immovable in every storm. He is your Lord, and your enemies are His footstool. You have no problem. You have no dilemma. You have no vice or stronghold that He cannot or will not overcome in you, through you, for you, or before you.

He is Jesus, and He is the Christ, the Son of the Living God. To Him a day is like a thousand years and a thousand years is like a day. He waits to hear from you today, that you may be girded and empowered to face what lies before you. The Lifter of Your Head wishes to gently elevate your expectations of His Presence in your life to be manifested in such a way that you enjoy the fullness of being eternally bound to your Bondservant. Christ is sufficient this day and every day. Behold a level of magnificence and grandeur warranted by and reserved only for Him.

When I behold Your grandeur, I behold ever-increasing, consecrated Supremacy. Yet even as your Supremacy increases, your accessibility never diminishes. I behold You, and I behold my undeserved access to You. As my awe of You increases, Your blood provides me with an even bolder access to Your throne of grace. You astound me! Amen.

DAY 15
Behold His Affection

God can testify how I long for all of you with the affection of
Christ Jesus.
Philippians 1:8

Christ took on flesh. He became flesh and made His dwelling among us.

You are not called to ignore your flesh but to celebrate it as Christ celebrates His. In Christ, you are to touch hearts in a spiritual sense while also touching them in a physical sense. Have you the presence of mind to pat another on the back when a pat on the back is what they may need most in that moment? Can we afford to be so spiritually minded that we neglect to offer an encouraging physical touch? Someone needs a hug today! A hug can mean more to them than we may realize. Some have gone "hugless" for decades. They need a holy touch.

You have, in Christ, the presence of mind to be a physical presence for another. A holy touch can reap a harvest of camaraderie. Who feels left out, overlooked, and unappreciated today? Perhaps a pause to share an embrace is paramount. Who needs a physical touch but has yet to even fully recognize that need?

Likewise, who might be better untouched? In Christ, you walk in discernment and in the acknowledgement that there is a great deal of pain in this broken world. You remain aware of the importance of discerning what others may need—or not need—from you. Are you not a priest and minister of the Lord? How are you approaching others today? Haphazardly? Or compassionately, with great sensitivity and respect?

Our Lord drank of a cup and hung on a tree and made fires and cooked fish because He knows that physical things matter. What would the Eucharist be without a tangible cup and edible bread? He created us to appreciate the tangible. He knows what a "holy kiss" is, and He knows when we need affirmation and validation when we are down.

In Christ, you lay hands on others for the impartation of the Spirit. Surely you will impart love and healing today through physical touch. You will know who needs a manifest expression of the Lord's love through a touch from you today. You lay hands on others to identify with needs. What physical needs has the Lord met in your life? Who might you touch today in a way that assures that person that you understand, that you recognize where they are today because you have been there?

Your spirit is clothed in flesh, not unlike our Lord, who took on flesh. Be the hugger you know He was and is. Be the back-patter you know He was and is today. Identify with another while you impart wisdom and encouragement. Minister to the whole person and love the Lord your God with all your heart and all your mind and all your strength. Love your neighbor in word and in deed, with sensitivity. You yourself love affection. Your Lord is affectionate when affection is what you need. Your Lord is the Son of the Most High God. Is He not affectionate because His Father is affectionate? Our Father, which art in heaven, hallowed be thy Name! When an earthly father withholds affection, our heavenly Father shares the affection of Christ Jesus. Be His hands, His feet. Embrace. Encourage. Share His affection.

How will God testify concerning your level of earnest affection? Will your Lord testify that you long to be with others?

How will He testify of how you shared affection today? Some are alone, and some are also lonely. Will He not place them in your path? In Christ, you have eyes to see the hearts of those in need of affection. You can sense in them a hunger to connect, make friends, and be included. You are a walking, feeling, and thinking disciple of Christ who looks after your own needs but also after the needs of others. Today, in Christ, behold His affection…and behold those to whom you should extend His affection.

When I need Your nearness most, You are there. Help me draw near to You, as I know You will draw near to me. I have need of the affection of Christ Jesus so that, in turn, I may be affectionate to others. Hug me. Encourage me. Show me Your affection, that I may embrace and encourage others—even the least among us. Amen.

DAY 16
Behold His Undivided Attention

We must pay the most careful attention, therefore,
to what we have heard, so that we do not drift away.
Hebrews 2:1

Your Lord affords you His undivided attention; you, in turn, bless others by giving them attention that is whole, holy, and respectful.

In a frenetic world, you are uniquely attentive. In a preoccupied world, you possess the special ability to be present. In a multitasking world, you make it your task to take time to respectfully listen to others. In a double-minded world, you, in Christ, are singularly focused. In the moments when you visit with another, he or she becomes the single most important individual in the world.

Each passing second, you are anointed to demonstrate respect to others. You rarely *spend* time with people; you *invest* time. You invest careful attention because you care. In Christ, you care about things that others have yet to even consider.

A house divided against itself cannot stand. You make every effort to keep the unity of the Spirit through the bond of peace. You understand unity's critical nature because you know the power of focus and oneness. You obviously understand the importance of being of one heart and one mind with others. You demonstrate obedience to God's call to oneness when interacting

62

with your fellow man. In Christ, you comprehend through experience the vital gravity of undivided attention.

As a Christian, you love others, you love your Lord, and you are mindful of each person in every conversation. You are divinely dialed in. You have an ear that listens to life-giving reproof. You dwell among the wise. You can hear words as well as the emotions behind them. You care, and you show it. You refrain from giving answers until you have actively listened; you avoid impulsive conversational folly. You listen with your eyes; they look directly forward, your gaze moves straight ahead. You know how to patiently ponder. Many are absent, but you are present.

You eagerly desire spiritual gifts. You have little difficulty discerning truth over fallacies. You can recognize falsehoods because you remain attentive and aware. You recognize opportunities when others see only inconvenience. You let others finish speaking before you begin your response.

In a world of inattentiveness, you are empathetic. In Christ, you can even hear in silence. The absence of words is not the absence of communication. Even in the absence of sound, a still, small voice of affirmation resonates in your heart. You are a skilled listener. Before you speak, you listen. Before you act, you listen. Before you invest, you listen. Before you teach, you listen. You are an adept, sensitive listener—to your Lord and to other people. You have eyes to see and ears to hear what the Spirit is saying to you, both directly and through others.

There is an art to listening, and you are growing in it. When someone is with you, that person senses that all of you is present. Face-to-face conversation is a dying art form in which you are an up-and-coming artist. In a screen-immersed world, you screen yourself from distractions. You are wholly present in an unholy world. You are uncommonly aware. You extinguish any superficiality in your interactions, and you remove any masks, choosing instead to communicate genuinely, even when it is costly.

You are improving and growing in your ability to give your undivided attention to others. When seeking the Lord, you offer more and more of your heart, your soul, and your undivided attention to Him, actively pursuing Him with greater and greater intensity.

When you are with others, they get with the best of you in that moment. You connect. You are highly favored because your singularity of mind and focus speaks to others of their value. Many wish to speak with you because they need to be heard, and they know you are attentive. Today you are present and ready to care. Behold your attentive Lord, and behold the people He places before you. Your undivided attention to them can speak louder than your words.

Your keen gift of observation and attention has elevated you in the favor of God and man.

———————————

Lord, You are the One that affords me Your undivided attention. Anoint me to that end for others, so that wherever I am, I am fully present. Tend to my heart and tenderize it to be single-minded in a multitasking world. Amen.

DAY 17
Behold Your Overflow

*May the God of hope fill you with all joy and peace as you
trust in him, so that you may overflow with hope by the power
of the Holy Spirit.*
Romans 15:13

Hope is the confidence that what you have been believing your
Lord for is in process, likely on the way, and soon to be. You
have confidence, you have assurance, and you have hope. Your
faith has precipitated your hope, hope that will ultimately foster
and accelerate a greater, deeper love.

Your hope has a God. No other god can provide hope; only
your God. Your Lord provides you with sure hope, hope that
originates in Him, not a false and disappointing hope that is
derived from a false god. Your faith is sure; therefore, your hope
is pure.

In Christ, your hope looks for cavities to fill. Your hope is a
divine caulk filling cracks and crevices within an expectant heart.
Your trust in Him fills your heart with joy and peace. Just the
thought of fulfilled hope fills your heart. Your heart has a fill
line.

Your mind, too, had rendered such a line, but it was errantly
drawn. Your Lord dismisses this kind of counterfeit "fill line"
based on fleshly capacity, past experiences, and a shallow, not-
yet-mature understanding of the God of hope.

66

Your true God of hope is reckless in His filling. He pours. He douses. He lavishes. He saturates. His love flows and runs over. Yes, He is the Lord of the Overflow, a torrent of hope filling and cascading over your heart as it plunges you into new levels of robust and refreshing hope. Hope away! He can and will deliver.

Hope is not simply a feeling or even merely an assurance. Hope comes by way of a waterfall that generates power. Your hope is electric—not for feelings' sake, but for power, the power of the Holy Spirit. Your faith, rooted in love, generates a hope overflow that can power an entire grid. Your hope overflows beyond what you can personally process. You often find yourself with excessive hope. This extravagant hope is not wasteful, for there are people around you who are living in a drought. For them, even a trickle of hope would be like your waterfall experience. They are parched as they exist in an arid desert of hopelessness. Your excess, your overflow of unbridled hope, is for them.

In Christ, you share your hope. You present hope, you speak of hope, you gift hope. You are a sworn-in, testifying eyewitness of the mist that rises from the waterfall of hope that you cannot yourself contain. Your mustard seed of faith has resulted in a waterfall of hope. Your disproportionately generous God proves to be excessive enough for you to describe. Your hope causes others to ponder the deluge of possibilities that lie just beyond their life-numbing idolatry.

The Person of the Spirit is personable to you, experiential to you. You are inhabited by a waterfall of hope. There is within you a river that wells up and overflows as a torrent of hope.

You can also be a sprinkler, a deliverer of an overflow of hope, at whatever capacity necessary, to irrigate and nourish almost-dead spiritual vegetation. You deliver that which is required to deliver others from hopelessness.

What an incredible calling to be a gardener tending to the vineyard of the Lord in the midst of a drought! Where you go, life goes. You are a vessel overflowing with living water. See yourself as you should. See yourself as a waterfall; by so doing, you will not hesitate to share the hope you have with others. The God of hope has filled you to overflowing so He may see His power at work through you to infuse an entire grid of hopeless people. Through you, He can irrigate an entire valley of bone-dry souls longing for spiritual rain. Behold it. You must see it and let Him overflow through you.

Make and keep me, Your servant, a mobile waterfall of hope welling up from the river of life within me. May I overflow with hope by the power of the Holy Spirit. Amen.

DAY 18
Behold the Mystery

Have nothing to do with godless myths and old wives' tales; rather, train yourself to be godly.
1 Timothy 4:7

Many speak of good luck and bad luck. But you know your life is more than chance or happenstance or an old wives' tale. Randomness cannot rule in your life, for randomness pales in comparison to the sovereignty of Christ your Lord. Serendipity may have its romantic allure, but it is not worthy of your dependence and trust.

It is not by chance your Lord created you. It is not by chance that you know Him…and that you now have the chance to make Him known. Riches are discovered in Him, not in some lottery. You are no accidental experiment but an ordained, pre-named, pre-known living being with the divine calling to willfully worship the One True God.

He supersedes statistics. He has power over probabilities. Nothing is random or unintentional concerning His life and ministry. He did not die on a random cross only to be buried in a random tomb and then rise on a random day. He embodies the word "purposeful."

In Christ, you have a purpose that is not defined by ups and downs and random respites but by a methodical, patient, orderly, and loving God who wants every bit of your heart.

70

You live an ordained life, and you live it with authority and gusto. Your destiny is in no way dependent upon chance or superstition. You need no luck at all, for to need such is to need Him less. He is all you need. He is all you could ever truly want.

He has plans for you, plans to prosper you. What He has for you is for your good, for your welfare, for your well-being. In Him, you have a hope and a future that is not dependent upon luck or fortune but solely upon His sovereignty.

Even now, He is preparing a place for you. Even now, He is prepared to return for you. No superstition could ever delay that coming, and no luck could ever hurry it. He is sure, decisive, and without variation or shadow or shifting. He is your Sovereign. Today He calls you by the name He gave you before you were born. He calls you to enjoy Him and to trust in His leading. Today He will establish your steps as you converse with Him.

He is knowable and accessible, but He remains, in part, a mystery. Your finite mind will not, cannot, this side of heaven, possess the capacity to fully know Him. He is by no means mythical, but for now He will, in some ways, remain appropriately mysterious.

Only through prayer can anyone fearlessly make known the mystery of the gospel. His gospel is revelatory and liberating. His gospel can make its way into an already-resistant heart and transform that heart at a mysteriously profound level. His gospel is as mysteriously profound as the covenantal bond between Christ and His church.

The Holy Eucharist remains profoundly and reverentially mysterious. Enjoy the mystery of Christ's blood—the wine; Christ's body—the bread.

Profoundly mysterious, too, is that you, together with all God's holy people, can begin to grasp the width and length and height and depth of the love of Christ. As mysterious and complex as such high doctrine might be, equally mysterious is His unchangeable love for you.

When put to song in the simplest of ways, the mystery of His love can be sung by a little child and lose not one iota of profundity or mystery. These lyrics remain equally profound for you today: "Jesus loves me, this I know, for the Bible tells me so."

Dispense of worldly explanations that minimize and marginalize Christ. He is and will remain a mystery until we see Him face to face, for until then, the Creator cannot fully be understood by His creation. Enjoy the mystery of trusting in your Sovereign. Train yourself to be godly, but leave ample room for the mysterious.

If I have cheapened You, Lord, forgive me. If I have discounted You, please forgive me. You are knowable, but my ability to fully know You this side of heaven is limited. Remain appropriately mysterious to me, Lord, for You are mysteriously sacramental. I am grateful that You know I need to be astounded by You. Amen.

DAY 19
Behold Your Substance

But he who did not know, yet committed things deserving of stripes, shall be beaten with few.
For everyone to whom much is given, from him much will be required; and to whom much has been committed, of him they will ask the more.
Luke 12:48 (NKJV)

Many gravitate toward the lowest common denominator. You, however, in Christ, strain to live up to a higher, uncommon calling. In Him, you strive to live to a standard that necessitates leaning in to and upon Him. You pursue excellence—not for accolades, but as the appropriate praise to your King. You refuse to be petty and infantile. You live a transcendent life in which there is little to no time for whining and complaining. In fact, you do all things without complaining. You hold out the word of truth as you shine like a star in the universe. People observe you and see an absence of desperate nonsense. You are no spiritual infant crying for attention; no, you are a seasoned example of how to rise above culture, sin, and worldliness. You live with poise, not for drama. You will not manipulate others or speak ill of others behind their backs. Your appetite is for the substance of the Bread of Life, not for trivial gossip. You have a resilience to conforming to any pattern of this world that is fleshy, base, and ultimately ridiculous.

74

You have the world on your heart, but you will not be worldly. You will not sit very long in the seat of mockers, if at all. Much has been given to you. Much is required of you. You have the Divine Presence at the ready to help you rise above that which longs to take you down. You are quick to be open to correction, and you will not defend childishness; neither will you condemn others who have yet to taste the transcendent life of Christ. Your witness is quiet, consistent, effective, and enjoyable. Nothing transcends your walk—not worldliness, not politics, not anything. He is first, all else is second. You care for the world as Christ cares for the world. You walk in holiness because, in Him, you are whole. Your life rises above all that seeks to bring others lower. If you catch yourself mimicking others at the expense of following Christ, you quickly recognize the difference, and you act upon it. You choose not to put another down to raise yourself up. You will not trade insult for insult.

In Him, you seek things above. In Him, you are seated in heavenly places. Your words are gracious and seasoned with salt. In Him, you set an example for believers in speech, in life, in love, in faith, in purity. When you were a child you spoke like a child, you thought like a child, you reasoned like a child. You are no longer a child. You speak with a voice that has a distinctive inflection; its timbre is unique and refreshing. Your desires are different. Your thoughts are of things that are praiseworthy, righteous, excellent, perfect, lovely, admirable, noble, and true.

In Him, you think and speak and live in a transcendent fashion because you are being fashioned by a different Potter on a different wheel than those in the world. You are in the world, but you are not of it. You have a sensitivity to gravitating to the "low" while longing for things above. You are pleasantly distinguishable from others. You are slow to speak and quick to listen. Your righteousness is not haughty, but loving and infectious. You spark a curiosity in others who yearn to break out of the penitentiary of pettiness. Your thoughts are not the world's thoughts, nor are the world's ways your ways. In Him, you seek a transcendence that comes from being called from deep unto deep. In Him, you are complete; you lack nothing. Your willing submission to your Lord is not self-demeaning, but Christ-exalting. You obey Him because you love Him, just as He obeyed the Father out of love for Him. You have resolve and spiritual and social integrity.

Lord, plant Your Word deep in my heart. Hide it there that I might not sin against You. May the depth and growth of Your Word in my heart reflect the breadth of my loving ministry to others. Amen.

DAY 20
Behold Christ Your Keel

The men were amazed and asked, "What kind of man is this?
Even the winds and the waves obey him!"
Matthew 8:27

A keel is the lowest point of a boat's hull; it is a boat's backbone. The keel provides strength and stability and prevents sideways drift.

As a treacherous storm raged about a boat filled with His terrified disciples, Jesus slept in the vessel's stern. Although the storm's manifestation was perilously real, Jesus was at peace. His own presence provided the strength and stability needed to weather the tempest.

Christ is your Keel in times of crisis, trial, insecurity, and fear. He is your backbone, your sustenance, and He keeps you from the dangers of the sideways drift. Behold Christ: "Even the winds and the waves obey Him!" Fear not, for He is with you.

You are not immune to an occasional sense of impending doom. Surely you know the discomfort of the piercing talons of uneasiness. A sense of looming dread may slither round about you, wanting to attach itself to your thoughts. Angst has its agenda, too; it longs to catch up with you, to chat about what is going on and, yes, what is going wrong. Angst positions itself to whisper to you late in the night when, in the silence, it has your undivided attention.

Many are fraught with an ongoing, abiding sense of havoc, but there is something distinctively unusual about you. You are no easy prey. You catch such thought patterns early, as your discernment quickly detects wrong turns in your mind's travel. You will not take such an errant exit off the road already ordained for you. You recognize that you must not be the victim of rehearsed apprehension, worry, or fear that is accompanied by a preoccupation with potential doom.

You know that you do not walk alone, that the Lord is your Helper. You will not fear or be

waylaid by something as destructive as Anxiety and its cousin, Worry. Tribulation may abound in your life, but in the midst of the storm, you have been given an abiding peace. Your peace is found in a Person once described as the Prince of Peace, but who has since ascended His throne to be known as our Sovereign King.

Take heart! He, now in you, has overcome the world! He is your hiding place, your citadel of protection from vain and empty worry. Should you allow Him, He will protect you. Look around. Listen closely. You are surrounded not by enemies but by songs of deliverance. Relax. He is at work and is dealing with the very source of your preoccupation and fixation. When the cares of your heart are many, His consolations cheer your soul. Why be downcast and miss the blessing of seeing His surprising, chivalric intervention? Your Prince is now your King. He rides on a white horse, ever mindful of your predicament and most enthusiastic about your imminent release from any constricting and asphyxiating fear that might result from it.

Gently release your cares; in fact, go ahead and cast them upon Him. He will answer you. He will deliver you. He cares for you. Your self-constructed prison, built with steely worry, is about to be unlocked. It is for freedom that Christ has set you free! Walk with a new sense of divine trust and confidence. Be anxious for nothing and be hopeful in everything. Do not entertain runaway panic but, in a stealthy stillness, surrender to your Keel who keeps you steady and safe and protected in the midst of the storm. Let your Lord do something in you, around you, and through you that will leave you lacking an ability to fully understand or articulate the peace He brings you. Be not anxious for tomorrow, but long for Him today. Managing today's concerns will be sufficient. Today is where you learn. Today is where you live. Today is satisfying.

"Let not your heart be troubled." Believe in the Father. Believe in the Son. Expect the Spirit's intervention. Consider your trials pure joy as others feebly run from the slithering source of paralyzing ineffectiveness. When intense trouble finds you, call on the name of the Lord. He is the one who answers by fire.

Remain confident, for your Keel is tested and found strong, able to keep you from the dangers of a problematic spiritual drift.

"Even the wind and the waves obey Him!"

Lord, I have the tendency to magnify a crisis at Your expense. I pray for the poise to magnify You over and above any challenges You allow to come my way. I want to truly magnify You for who You are first, not what You can do for me.
Amen.

DAY 21
Behold Your High Pursuit

And without faith it is impossible to please God,
because anyone who comes to him must believe that he exists
and that he rewards those who earnestly seek him.
Hebrews 11:6

There are many opportunities to chase things in this life. In Christ, you are first a "God chaser." You get it. You get the need to transcend the all-too common with a healthy, balanced pursuit of God and all He has for you. Spiritual vigor is a means to spiritual growth. Spiritual vigor leads to emotional stability. Spiritual vigor leads to physical well-being. Spiritual vigor overcomes tepid, loveless relationships.

If one cannot or will not be passionate toward the One who bore their sins, shouldn't passion be redefined? In Christ, you are in passionate pursuit of the One True God, and He is a rewarder of those who diligently seek Him. Passionless Christianity is an oxymoron. Passionless Christianity is reason for concern.

You are a seeker of God. You are a seeker of truth. You won't ever be truly settled until you settle into a daily, intentional pursuit of God. Refuse to settle for what this world has to offer. Remember:

In Christ, you earnestly seek Him—yet He Himself is the reward. Pursue Him.

In Christ, your fervor for God must exceed the false satisfaction offered by the world. Be passionate for Him.

In Christ, your desire to behold Him must exceed the distractive pull of this world. Prioritize Him.

Your recognition of the critical importance of pursuing Christ must exceed the clamor and confusion of this world, which keeps you from Him. Settle not.

This world tenaciously seeks to alienate you from your pursuit of Christ. The wares of this world are paraded before you daily, inviting you into a mesmerizing stupor that creates an illusion of the fullness of Christ. Do not settle for less than He offers you. Do not forsake your first love. Be bound to Him today.

Your Lord has seated you in the heavenly realms with every spiritual blessing in Christ. Don't just seek Him—seek Him with all your heart. Seek Him while He may be found. Come boldly to His throne of grace to obtain mercy. He has a master plan for you; He wants to prosper you and keep you from harm, self-inflicted or otherwise.

As you keep your Lord high and lifted up, remain in high pursuit of the One you love. Fulfill His high calling on your life. Seek Him, and seek first His kingdom and His righteousness.

You have been raised with Christ. Set your heart on things above, where Christ is, seated at the right hand of God. Set your mind on things above, not on earthly things. For you—the old you—died, and your life is now hidden with Christ in God. When Christ, who is your life, appears, then you also will appear with Him in glory. Put to death, therefore, what is earthly in you: sexual immorality, impurity, lust, evil desire, and greed, which is idolatry. Settle not. Settle not. Settle not. But be settled in Him. He loves you so, and He desires to have an ongoing, reciprocal pursuit of you.

Seek Him; you will find Him when you seek Him with all your heart. Until your whole heart can truly seek Him, seek Him with what you have. Be sincere in your pursuit. Engage Him in conversation. Douse Him with worship. Bring your curiosity before Him. Exclude no subject. Trust and vulnerability are your friends. Reverence is your transport, and Christ is your Way. Come to the Father today, through the Son. His yoke is easy, and His burden is light.

Seek Him. Settle not.

Father, I thank You that goodness and mercy are following me all the days of my life. May goodness and mercy encourage me to always pursue You, Your kingdom, and Your righteousness first. You are my High Pursuit. Amen.

DAY 23
Behold His Simplicity

He grew up before him like a tender shoot,
and like a root out of dry ground.
He had no beauty or majesty to attract us to him,
nothing in his appearance that we should desire him.
Isaiah 53:2

In this world are many simpletons. Simpletons lack understanding. They have great need of knowledge yet to be acquired. Simpletons even avoid the process of learning.

In this world, there are many fools. Fools lack reverence for the Divine and, with such a deficit, they lack wisdom.

In this world are many mockers, those who blatantly scoff at truth and, in arrogance, proclaim their self-defined superiority.

In this world, there are geniuses, people bloated with knowledge but lacking faith.

In this world, there is also great confusion, increasing fear, and abounding deception.

This world system often breeds complexity, but it is a simple fact that greater is He that is in you than he that is in the world.

In Christ, you are not of this world. You are but a sojourner passing through into eternity. Your citizenship is in heaven. You are no simpleton, for you have the mind of Christ. Although you deeply understand the need for simplicity, you are no simpleton.

In this complicated world, you understand the value of simplicity. You comprehend the simplicity of submission. You recognize a holy command from God, and you understand the simplicity of both obeying that command out of love and embracing His grace when such a command is broken. You have no need for rationalizing your behavior for your own justification. You are already justified in Christ; it's as simple as that. You approach life and your Lord with a childlike faith while others childishly strut about atop a Tower of Babel made by their own hands.

Yes, in Christ, you launch into your day with one simple priority: to seek first the kingdom of God. You seek God in all things. You reap the rewards that come from simply and diligently seeking your Lord. To you, simplicity in ministry is both essential and vital. Life is not increasingly complex; rather, it is increasingly simple for you. The more you mature, the simpler your approach to life is. Your reflection on the truth of the Word only heightens your simple desire to follow Christ. The Holy Spirit whispers explanations to you that are sorely needed and adequately simple yet dependable, rich, and rock solid.

In Christ, you can articulate the gospel to all people in ways that are simple and easy to understand. Your ministry, like your Lord's, is steeped in simplicity. Anything around you can be used to explain the loving devotion of your Lord. You can seek wisdom from children and make known the mysteries of the gospel. You are a harbinger of spot-on, candid simplicity that promotes in others a clarity of thought. Your simple, righteous approach to life breeds comfort in them as they seek to understand His remarkable peace that transcends all understanding.

Too often, a complex approach to the things of God is but a hiding place from actually doing the work of the ministry. When you actively love and serve others (the actual call of Christ to those who would follow Him), you lack no depth at all. Pontificating upon the Scripture has its place, but it will never be a replacement for serving the least among us.

You, with childlike simplicity, talk directly with your Lord more than you talk about Him. You are okay with being a tender shoot, and you are quite satisfied worshiping One. The simplicity of the human heart's ability to demonstrate love and compassion is majestic. Why would Christ need to appear outwardly majestic? Was His beauty limited to an outward appearance? Of course not. People are far more attracted to Him by His inner beauty.

Trust on, soldier of Christ. Emulate our Lord, who remained focused, relatable, and simply simple in His approach to ministering to His people who swim in a sea of complexity. Walk out His orders and enjoy the victory and joy of simplistic obedience and His never-ending love.

O Lord, infuse me with the wisdom to mature today. At the same time, would You preserve a childlikeness in me while keeping me from childishness? Show me please, how to discern the complexities of this world while retaining the simplicity of just being Yours. Amen.

DAY 24
Behold Knowing Christ

I want to know Christ—yes, to know the power of his resurrection and participation in his sufferings, becoming like him in his death, and so, somehow, attaining to the resurrection from the dead.
Philippians 3:10–11

Not everyone is blessed by a revelation that gives them a fresh, invigorating way of approaching this life and the life to come. Revelations that originate in flesh and blood decay and die in eternity.

You have a divine revelation of Christ that originated not in any man or woman; this revelation directly emanated from your Source of Life. It began with eternity in mind. An eternal perspective is essential to fully appreciate the ongoing revelation of truly knowing the multifaceted brilliance and splendor of your Lord.

Satan may seek to oppress you, but you have already been possessed by the life-giving Lord, Jesus Christ. In Him, the revelation you have received has indescribable depth and eternal impact. Yes, Someone—not something—has been revealed to you. You see Christ not simply as historical or theoretical, but as the personal, personable Son of the Living God.

Your revelation of Christ is steeped in rich warmth, marinated in empathy, and glazed with genuine concern. You are no servant of a theoretical god; you are a friend of your very Creator. Your walk is, in every respect, personal. Your spiritual life can ill afford to be mechanical or merely rhetorical. You simply want to know Christ in an ever-increasing manner. Yes, as wonderful as your revelation is, a revelation alone does not a seasoned friendship make.

Your initial revelation of Christ is foundation enough to begin building the kingdom of God where you live and move and have your being. But that revelation of Christ to you is steadily and increasingly growing. As your love for and commitment to Him builds and as you grow in relationship with Him, the revelation of Christ that is being built on that foundation adds height and structure and beauty. The more He reveals to you of Himself, the broader His influence through you becomes. Your revelation is only beginning. Its picture frame is borderless. Your revelation of Christ is thriving, widening; it is becoming sharper, clearer, and more attractive and compelling. Christ is ever so carefully revealing His heart to you. He is wooing you and, in so doing, provoking in you greater thought and deeper understanding. You want to know Christ and the power of His resurrection. In Him, you even want to know a fellowship with Him in the midst of suffering. You want to become more like Him in death, yet you want Him to live through you more in life.

Like freshly baked bread, your revelation of Christ has a fragrance of worship round about it. Trials clarify the boundlessness of His strength and dependability. In trials, His revelation of Himself to you is cause for joy! Your revelation of your Lord is expanding. He is building upon your ever-improving revelation of His covenantal faithfulness.

You are a learner and a leaner. You learn from Him, and you lean into Him as needed. You are learning as you seek to know Him more. You are leaning into Him as you experience challenges that require you to trust Him more. The greatest risk you can take is to stop wanting more of Him. No, regardless of your season in your walk with Christ, you want to know Him and the power of His resurrection. That which He reveals to you, you refuse to conceal from others. As He increases your understanding of Him today, and as you share that insight with others, He multiplies your experience in their hearts.

You long for a revelation of Christ that, day by day, increases your comprehension as to the height, depth, and breadth of the love of Christ. Upon that rock He will build His church, and the gates of hell cannot and will not prevail against it.

Ask Him for an ongoing desire to know Him and share Him with others. You can know Him and the power of His resurrection. Behold the gift of knowing Him.

I truly want to know You in a richer way. I want to know the power of Your resurrection. May that same power be reflected in my attitude and my love for others. Your perfect love casts out fear; help me have no timidity when it comes to sharing Your gospel, as it is Your power. If I know You better, I will love others more. Amen.

DAY 25
Behold Your Guzzler

"Father, if it is Your will, take this cup away from Me;
nevertheless not My will, but Yours, be done."
Then an angel appeared to Him from heaven, strengthening
Him.
Luke 22:42–43(NKJV)

In this world, people worship many idols. Idols are without life. They have no blood. Idols are without laughter and void of compassion or joy. Idols have no passion. They lack understanding; they're unable to give or receive love. Idols cannot purchase anyone's redemption through self-sacrifice, for they cannot die since they were never alive. Idols exist to draw you away from Christ, the Son of the Living God.

You know that life is found in the blood. You have crossed the bloodline. You have crossed the threshold from spiritual death into life. Only by the blood of the Lamb do you have eternal pulse and vibrancy. He has purchased you with His blood. You are His. You were bought at a great price, not with perishable things such as silver or gold, but with the precious blood of Christ, like that of a lamb without blemish. No ransom, no premium so high has ever been paid, nor will it ever be again.

The church is His, bought by His blood. Behold the Lamb of God, "looking as if it had been slain." Walk in the light as He is in the light…and the blood of Jesus will purify you from all sin.

94

He began bleeding on your behalf at Gethsemane. It was there that the Father began to impress upon Christ, your Scapegoat, the crucifixion ahead. The Father began pressing the sin of the world into the Son. Your Scapegoat became one with your sin—though He was without sin. He took your blood-bought sin outside the camp, away from you, that you may be judged as righteous.

Christ is your Navigator. He is your Bright and Morning Star. Your Lord is your True North.

By His blood, He separated you from your sin as far as the east is from the west. Jesus the Christ is your Faithful Witness. His blood marks you; His blood speaks on your behalf.

Christ is no idol. He first lived and He then died, and then He rose to life again. He, even now, ever liveth to make intercession for you. He hung in your place so you could stand in His righteousness.

Death passes over those with the blood of the Lamb on the doorpost of their hearts. Death, where is thy sting? O grave, where is thy victory? The blood of Christ speaks for you. The blood of Christ covers you. The blood of Christ atones for you. The blood of Christ redeems you, justifies you, insulates you, and protects you. The blood is, even now, sanctifying you. You shall overcome by the power of the blood of the Lamb and the word of your testimony.

Your anguished Christ sought His Father in the Garden of Gethsemane: "Father, if it is Your will, take this cup away from Me; nevertheless not My will, but Yours, be done." Upon receiving His Father's answer, He had to make a decision.

Would He willingly drink the cup of suffering? Yes, not only would He drink of the cup, but He was also poured out like a drink offering in the process.

"Father, if it is Your will, take this cup away from Me; nevertheless not My will, but Yours, be done." Christ surrendered to His Father's will. Then an angel appeared to Him from heaven, strengthening Him.

Followers of Christ reverently and ceremonially sip from a cup of redemption, careful not to spill and stain. Delicately, the bread—the body of Christ—makes its way to one's tongue, and there it is neatly perched before being consumed.

At the very thought of consuming the cup and being ravaged in the process, your Christ bled. We sip in a span of only seconds. For an entire afternoon, He guzzled the miry bog of human depravity, spilling upon Himself the stain and stench of human sin in a once-and-for-all gluttonous encounter with the worst part of every one of us.

Behold Holiness defiled. Behold the blemished Lamb. Behold your Scapegoat. Behold your Guzzler. Be still and know that He is God.

———————————

I know You want to reason with me, Lord. Though my sins are like scarlet, they have, through Your blood, become whiter than snow. I find the reasoning difficult. I find the mystery bewildering. And I find You worthy of all praise and glory and honor. I love You. Amen.

DAY 26
Behold His Silence

He was oppressed and afflicted,
yet he did not open his mouth;
he was led like a lamb to the slaughter,
and as a sheep before its shearers is silent,
so he did not open his mouth.
Isaiah 53:7

Silence can have within it inherent purpose and power. Silence, the contextual atmospheric context for the creation of the world, is also the divine envelope in which the spoken Word of God is delivered. Silence is the clean palette from which the colorful revelation of Christ is painted.

In Christ, you are growing in your discernment of the power of the unsaid. Some scenarios are only cheapened by words, as your Lord knows full well. Immediately before His shearers, disfigured as He was, He silenced Himself. You understand that words can at times rob the Almighty of His greatest platforms from which to speak directly to the hearts of men and women. In the solemnity of silence, in a context for which words remained inadequate, a Roman Centurion—an otherwise hardened executioner embraced by surety—received and declared the revelation that Christ Himself was the Son of God. Behold the silence of the Sheep before the shearers that gave birth to divine revelation.

As Jesus became increasingly one with the sin of the world, the pristine holiness of the Father had to turn away and forsake His own grossly marred and defiled Son. Christ, blaming no one, accusing no one, silenced any righteous and judicious self-defense within Him, only to be forsaken by His Father on your behalf. Christ was forsaken that you, in Him, will never be forsaken. His defilement ensured that you will never be plucked from the compassionate hand of the Father. He was forsaken; now, you are embraced. He was cursed and now you are liberated. Even as a once-clean Vessel, He became divinely adhered to every sin ever committed…and even then, He sinned not. Contaminated to the fullest possible extent, He manifested neither a whisper nor a hint of defiance, but only a strangely otherworldly statement: "Father, forgive them, for they know not what they do."

Behold His silence and follow accordingly. Speak not and cheapen not. Speak not and sin not. In Christ, you are fostering an earnest and appropriate silence before your King. Many grope for words to impress others; you know their sporadic inadequacy and limitations. Just be. Just be silent. Embrace the muteness befitting the presence of your King and be silent before Him.

You worship the One True God before whom, at times, the only appropriate response is silence. As your grasp of understanding the power of God intensifies, so too will your understanding of the need for strategic wordlessness in His presence. Be still and know that He is God. Be reverentially still and be enveloped by the meekness and tranquility of honorific quietness.

He was oppressed and afflicted, yet He did not open His mouth. He was silent before His accusers. Silent, but not helpless. No one took His life; He willingly laid it down in submission to His Father.

In Christ, your silence is becoming the forum in which the Spirit provokes deep thought concerning sin and salvation. You know when to speak and when to listen. You wisely discern when to open and when to close your mouth, as well as when to open and close your ears. You are a discerning and sensitive follower of Christ, ever recognizing both His voice and the need for silence.

The single most grotesque and unjust execution of life was peppered with thought-provoking silence. In Christ's silence before His shearers, all of humanity is afforded an opportunity to contemplate the greatest demonstration of love ever willingly chosen. The world's single greatest injustice prophetically ensured that you would be justified before the Father.

It wasn't in the earthquake or in the shifting cataclysmic anomalies that took place that day that God spoke the loudest. It was in the piercing silence that the Savior of the world chose to die for you.

And it is what the Lord did not speak aloud that still speaks today: the still, small, profound voice that says, "I love you."

Lord, at first, I found silence and stillness uncomfortable and sterile. Now I see silence and stillness as essential prerequisites to beholding You with awe. I know You will never leave me. My prayer is that my awe of You would never leave me, as well. When I truly behold You, Lord, I stand in awe of You. Continue to infuse me with a contagious, piercing awe of you, O God.
Amen.

DAY 27
Behold Christlessness

Therefore He says:
"When He ascended on high, He led captivity captive, and
gave gifts to men."(Now this, "He ascended"—what does it
mean but that He also first descended into the lower parts of
the earth? He who descended is also the One who ascended far
above all the heavens, that He might fill all things.)
Ephesians 4:8–10 (NKJV)

On that disturbing Friday night, those who had believed in Christ were at their lowest, while He descended to the lowest parts of the earth in order to lead captivity captive.

The temple was desecrated, ravaged. When the Holy of Holies was no longer holy, when the veil had been torn in two from top to bottom, Christ's followers moved from top to a new bottom themselves.

In a borrowed tomb lay the believing world's Hope for emancipation. The world was, for a brief period, seemingly Christless again. The prophetic arrival and life of the long-expected Messiah had abruptly been pulled, stretched, and ripped from them. The hearts of the people were empty, for the tomb was occupied. He had not saved Himself, though He could have. He was gone. In His peculiar, eerie absence, hope, too, seemed to be gone. No more teachings. No more miracles. No more amazement.

102

Do you not know what it feels like to think God Himself is dead?

As darkness approached, the world returned to the quiet preparations of a Sabbath meal, the prelude to a time of much-needed decompression. The apocalyptic events of that day, stunning as they were, had quickly yielded to the normalcy of another Sabbath night at home. The true

Source of Sabbath rest was dead, leaving His followers stunned, confused, and restless.

You were not there the day they crucified your Lord, but you now know the cross was a demonstration of His love. You live in a world void of the awareness of the true Source of hope. You live among those who may worship in some kind of temple, but one that is Christless, void of the manifest presence of the One True God.

In Christ, you are wise because you can empathize with the sense of Christlessness in others. You recognize that being down does not define them, but that it defines their need for the One who descended into the depths. You know not to determine the future based on circumstances or one's emotional reaction to them. You know your Lord is Faithful and True. You know to wait upon Him. You know to trust when others bust. The transactional payment for your soul has been finalized; it is non-returnable and never-changing. You are His. Even if it feels as though He has departed, even for a moment, you know He is coming back. He has promised to never leave you nor forsake you. You abide in Him, and He abides in you. On this side of heaven, there is no real Christlessness. Wherever you are today, and wherever you may go, He is in and with you. You are in Christ—inseparable—and you are in the victorious covenant He personally initiated and fulfilled. You do not need to see Him to know He has not left you. You are eternally His.

There is nothing holy about a torn veil, but there is something forever glorious about a permanently accessible throne room of grace. In Christ, you have irrevocable access to the Father. Even today, your prayers come before Him like incense. You have right of entry to the King's courts. Although Christ remains dead in the minds of many, His life in you—a living epistle—is readable by all. You point them to the only true Ever-Present Help in Time of Need, no longer dead but alive forevermore. Your life is a testimony to the veracity of the ever-so-relevant resurrection of Christ.

Live on.

Lord, in the midst of a gospel famine, how can I live without eternal food? Expand Your light in me; make it hotter and brighter. Grant me a burden for those around me who are listless, hopeless, and worshipless. May my burden for the lost far exceed the intensity of the selfishness required to ignore them. Amen.

DAY 28
Behold the Resurrection

"I am the resurrection and the life.
The one who believes in me will live, even though they die;
and whoever lives by believing in me will never die. Do you
believe this?"
John 11:25–26

Without the resurrection of Christ, Christianity is a false religion, led by apostate, false prophets and used by Satan to deceive the entire world. Yet, with the resurrection of Christ and the reality that He actually *is* the resurrection, we are a people with a substantive explanation for joy, hope, gratitude, newness of mind, and personal transformation.

The resurrection was not something that simply happened to Christ—or to a widow's son, to Lazarus, to a 12-year-old girl, or to a Shunammite woman's boy. Resurrection power is inseparable from Christ's essence and actions. Where He goes, so too goes resurrection power.

You are a dwelling place of His resurrection power. Resurrection power raises your hope, heightens your awareness, and lifts your spirit. His character and first inclination, as is yours, is to raise up. You build others up and offer them life as you live out the high calling of Christ for your life. You pick up when needed; you look up when tested, and you rise up when challenged. Resurrection power abides in you. It quickens you.

You know to elevate your ideas, your actions, and your influence for the kingdom. Behold Him Who is the Resurrection in thought, word, and deed. Look up, for your redemption draweth nigh.

In a world infused with morbidity and obsessed with liquidity, you rise above the common, the predictable, and the aimless. The "old you" was dead on delivery in your sins and transgressions, but the "new you" is fully alive, fully engaged, and fully intrigued with the kingdom of God, its divine architecture, and its splendor. You are enriched with a resurrected mindset, a regenerated vernacular, and a life renewed in the power of the Spirit. You are "a city set on a hill" that cannot be hidden as you interact with others and remain mindful of His equally high calling on their lives. Time spent with you is an investment, at a high yield, in the cause of Christ, our resurrection.

You are void of complaints and enveloped by purpose as you continue to lift Him high in your life. Everything in you looks and thinks upward. You climb up and away from gossip, you rise above lies and deception, you move ever higher than selfishness. You know that He exalts those who refuse to exalt themselves. You have seized the wisdom of exalting lowliness. You do not accept the temptation to remain down; you always move toward getting up. Resurrection best describes the accentuation of the risen Christ in you. In you, He can be seen as the glory and lifter of another's head. You gently elevate the downcast as you urge them to move in an otherworldly direction. You overcome deadly accusations, deadly shame, and deadly bitterness by immersing in the life-giving river of the Spirit Who flows upward and out of you.

Christ, the resurrection and the life, lives in you; therefore, resurrection abides in you and desperately longs to raise others up. Raise away! Behold the power of love and compassion. Overcome the stench of dead thinking, lifeless ambition, and a corpse-like approach to life. Behold and be infused with the *zōē* life of Christ...then infuse others.

May the power of resurrection become an active, contagious characteristic in your life. Look for the nearly-too-far-gone zombies of the world and resurrect them as new followers of the resurrected Christ. May you continue to never put others down, never operate below your potential, and never believe for less-than-mighty things.

Get up! Rise up! Lift up the name of Jesus, that He will draw all men to Himself. He is the resurrected King, the King above every king. He is the Name above every name.

Holy, Holy, Holy is the Lord God Almighty, who reigns in all the earth!

I pray for upward motion in my life, Lord. Please help me keep my thinking up, my attitude up, my generosity up, and my expectations of You up. Help me to be a lifter and a gifter. In an otherwise distracted and angry world, I pray for focus and poise. May the never-dissipating power of Your resurrection ever prompt me to get up, look up, and make up. Amen.

DAY 29
Behold the Ascension

*They were looking intently up into the sky as he was going,
when suddenly two men dressed in white stood beside them.
"Men of Galilee," they said, "why do you stand here looking
into the sky? This same Jesus, who has been taken from you
into heaven, will come back in the same way you have seen him
go into heaven."*
Acts 1:10–11

Atop the ark of the covenant, amid the glorious, manifest presence of God, is the mercy seat of God. There, two pristine angelic figures flank the ark, fixated on its contents. Within the ark is the budded staff of the first High Priest, Aaron, a golden jar of heavenly manna, and the Torah, the tablets of the law of God.

The day was growing long. The ravaged body of Jesus was prepared for burial. He was laid in a borrowed, empty tomb. On the third day, two angelic figures were seen in the area near the garden tomb, as though their assignment was to tend to the Lord Himself. Perhaps they had flanked the dead body of the Christ. Perhaps they had fixed their gaze upon Him, beholding the High Priest in the order of Melchizedek. Perhaps they remained still and beheld the Bread of Life, not unlike a jar of manna. If so, in so doing, they beheld the fulfillment of the law of God.

At the ascension of Christ, two men dressed in white stood with the apostles, the humble band of brothers representing the new church and tasked with building the kingdom of God. After He ascended, Christ sat down at the right hand of the Father. The Prince of Peace ascended the throne of the Father and became, on our behalf, the King of Kings. There, the two, because of God's abundant mercy, stayed flanked and affixed on the church of Jesus Christ.

You are the apple of God's eye. He sees you; He tends to you and keeps you as a shepherd and priest tends and keeps his flock. His staff is to your right; His rod is to your left. You have heavenly manna on which to dine. In Christ, you too have fulfilled the law of God. You stand on the Word of God. You are continually being chased by goodness and mercy.

Behold, you are flanked and entertained by strategically positioned angels, even though you may be unaware of their presence. Your Sovereign is aware of your coming and going. He knows your every need before you ask. Sitting at the right hand of God, at the right hand of power, is your King, who ever lives to intercede for you. You are resourced with all you will ever need to do what God is calling you to do. You too are the humble church embracing a lost and dying world. You live in a world suffering from a spiritual drought accompanied by a gospel famine. In that context, you are a source of living water and heavenly manna.

Behold your own need to ascend. Ascend to the next level of devotion, allegiance, and effectiveness. Ascend to the next grade in the school of relevant ministry. Ascend the hill of the Lord daily with clean hands and a pure heart. Ascend to your potential in Christ.

Many live in a dark spiritual night where it is cold and seemingly hopeless. As long as it is day, we must do His work. Night is coming when no one can work. So labor in the fields.

Behold, the fields are white and ready for harvest! Labor now on behalf of others. And behold, you too will be seated in heavenly realms with every spiritual blessing in Christ.

Share that blessing now. Sow the seeds of the gospel now. You entertain angels unaware. You are uniquely positioned to do great and mighty things which you do not know. Be still and know that He is God…but do not stay still, so others will know He is God, as well.

———————————

May I not be caught looking into the sky when I could be at work building Your kingdom. Lead me, Lord, to the right fields, the right workers, and the right-minded who want to see others ascend when they are otherwise descending, lost, and downtrodden. Help me ascend to my potential in You. Amen.

DAY 30
Behold, He is Coming Soon

"Look, I am coming soon!
Blessed is the one who keeps the words of the prophecy
written in this scroll."
Revelation 22:7

Your Lord has provided, for all of humankind, a clear, concise, direct promise: He is returning soon. Behold this promise. Behold the One making it, and correctly conclude that every believer within every generation is called to live and serve with an expectancy of the imminent return of the Messiah. No believer of any generation is completely ignorant of the possibility of His return in their lifetime. This promise is made known to all those who believe and are seeking to make Christ known, as well to those who have heard the promise and have yet to believe.

Christ is Truth, and what He says will come to pass. In that His promises are yes and amen, He will surely return soon! The Promise Keeper is coming soon. As is the custom, the Bridegroom has gone to Father's manor to prepare a place for His Bride; if it were not so, He would have told you.

Christ, the Word Keeper, has given His word: He is coming soon. He calls you to live as first-century believers lived, with the anticipation that He could return at any moment. Therefore, you live with the expectancy that today may be your last. You keep your word and you give His Word away. Your yes is yes and your no is no. In Christ, you do what you say you will do. You do not do what you said you will not do. Like Him, you live with integrity.

In the midst of a global gospel famine, you are a spiritual bakery. You walk about with warm loaf after warm loaf of the Bread of Life. You emit a spiritual fragrance akin to that of fresh-baked bread slathered with honey from the Rock. He is coming soon, and He'll bring with Him those you have fed. Feed people, for they are perishing for a lack of bread. You have come to realize you cannot live by physical bread alone but by every word that proceeds from the mouth of God. Give others this spiritual bread. You may think you have little to offer—perhaps only five small loaves, along with two small fish—yet you are in Christ; you are His ambassador of reconciliation. You have infinite fresh bread that never goes stale. You have eternal bread for the masses. Feed them, for soon, your Lord will return to see whom you have fed.

You may well live in a time people in other generations had longed to see: the time of the return of Jesus Christ. The train of the Lord surely filled the temple, but one day soon, you yourself will be the Lord's train that follows Him into a victorious battle over evil. You, dressed in white linen, will follow Him Who sits upon His white horse. Your Lord, called Faithful and True, will lead you and multitudes of believers into victory.

I saw heaven standing open and there before me was a white horse, whose rider is called Faithful and True. With justice he judges and wages war. His eyes are like blazing fire, and on his head are many crowns. He has a name written on him that no one knows but he himself. He is dressed in a robe dipped in blood, and his name is the Word of God. The armies of heaven were following him, riding on white horses and dressed in fine linen, white and clean. Coming out of his mouth is a sharp sword with which to strike down the nations. "He will rule them

with an iron scepter." He treads the winepress of the fury of the wrath of God Almighty. On his robe and on his thigh he has this name written:
KING OF KINGS AND LORD OF LORDS
Revelation 19:11–16

I am Yours, Lord. Help me to make others Yours, as well. Plant in me an urgency to stay at the epicenter of all You are doing in the lives of those around me. I have Bread to share; fill others as we fulfill Your great commission. Amen.

DAY 31
Behold Your Diamond

Be still before the Lord and wait patiently for him;
do not fret when people succeed in their ways,
when they carry out their wicked schemes.
Psalm 37:7

Still thyself. Just be. The multifaceted Christ can, in part, be likened to a brilliant diamond. Once you look to Him, His brilliant light will be reflected and appreciated by you. In your learned and acquired stillness, behold Him. In your gratitude, be beholden to Him in thanksgiving and worship.

Your personal Lord has become a Place; He is your Hiding Place. As you linger before Him, His intimate presence is your safe haven. He is your Keel, steadying you in times of crisis. Wait on Him in silence as He sings songs of deliverance over you. You are surrounded. Nothing can get in, and you surely do not want to get out. Linger in awe of your Lord. He is grand and inspiring. Having been cleansed by His redemptive blood, He invites you to experience the fullness of His joy.

Yes, be awed by Him in every way! He shares His power with you, to the extent that you might do even greater works than He. You have an anointing from the Holy One. He lights upon you with the sweetness of His Spirit so that you, His vessel, may set the captives free.

You are His manger. You literally and spiritually feed others. You empty yourself, and He fills you back up. You are His Bethlehem, His house of bread. Seek not to manage Him; when necessary, He manages you as you gratefully remain His manger.

Behold the Lamb that taketh away the sin of the world. Be reminded today that gentleness is a fruit of the Spirit. The meek shall inherit the earth. There is great strength in the essence of His complete humility and sacrificial love. Behold, there are many ways…but He is The Way. You are in Him; where He goes, you go. You abide in Him and He in you. You are no longer wayward, because you know Him—The Way.

Behold, He is The Truth. You speak truth, you teach truth, you eat and meditate on truth, you worship in Spirit and in truth. Truthfully, you are a mobile embassy of liberation, for just as the truth has set you free, you lead others to emancipation.

To a lost and dying world, Christ in you is Life. A hopeless, Christless world does not look for a "thought-to-be-dead" Savior. You carry the resurrected life of Christ within you. You are a visible, audible epistle to be read and heard by all those who have yet to come to know Him.

Behold, deep within you is a river that flows with great intensity. The God of excessive hope deepens and strengthens that river to cascade as a powerful, rushing waterfall that saturates those in your realm of influence. Your abundant hope is gleaned and lapped up by the hopeless. Your enthusiasm for life is like a mist shrouding that waterfall of hope.

Behold, in Christ, no day is exactly like another. Each day reveals a new facet or detail of Him, enabling you to continue to grow in wisdom and stature. You will not easily define or pigeonhole Him. You are learning to enjoy Him while allowing Him to remain, respectfully, a mystery, recognizing that you will never fully know your Lord until you see Him face to face. At times, you are mystified by the height, width, length, and depth of His love. Embrace the simplicity of a relationship with Him while also standing in the mystery of the gospel. Reverence the tangibility of the eucharist as well as the consecrated mystery of the cup. He is both simple and mysterious. Behold, you can want to know Him and the power of His resurrection while understanding you cannot know all of Him—not now.

Behold the "pursueability" of the Christ. Pursue the Rewarder of those who earnestly seek Him. Find Him and be taken aback by His attentiveness and affection. He loves you. He *is* love. He will never stop loving you. He loves you and, as your Lifeguard, He safeguards you. You are swimming in a pool of overly sufficient grace. You are basking poolside in the brilliance of knowing you now want Him more than you want sin. His grace is now more of an allure than is temptation. Of course you can rest now! You can rest and sleep now in the assurance that He is your rest and your Sabbath. He watches over you. He can even make you lie down in green pastures.

Be. And behold! Behold the substance of Christ. The deeper your walk with Him, the wider your ministry's impact. Let the Word dwell in you richly as you teach and admonish others in all wisdom. You have depth and resilience because He is your depth and resilience. You are courageous in crisis, and you remain poised in the present rather than anxious for the future. You have a Shepherd who impart a peace that mysteriously transcends your and anyone else's understanding.

Behold, your Lord guzzled a cup of suffering that you may dine at the table of the King, regenerated, cleansed, and ever more sanctified. He guzzled a miry bog on your behalf; though your sins be as scarlet, they shall be as white as snow.

Behold His silence on the cross while you relish your own. Before the shearers, silence. In the silence, we hear the voice that convicts and reveals truth within us all, the voice that did not defend Himself or blame any other.

Behold the high calling on your life. Are you not infused with the resurrection power of Christ? Are you not called to transcend the common, the ordinary, for the sake of Christ and for the Christless? You are called. You are consecrated. You are infused and resourced with divine confidence and power. Be a blameless and pure child of God in the midst of a wicked and depraved generation. You shall shine like a star in the universe as you hold out the Word of truth.

Behold, the day is coming when no man can work. He is coming soon! He is coming back for you, His bride, and He has prepared a place for you. Behold your King today. Still thyself. Behold the Lamb of God that taketh away the sin of the world, and worship Him. Raise Him up today, that He may draw all men to Himself.

Show me, Lord, the most fitting way to behold You today. Let me not behold anyone or anything at Your expense. Help me to simply be. Help me hold on to the horns of Your altar. Help me behold every aspect of Your nature. I fix my eyes on You today, Lord. Reveal all I need to see, know, and share with others. Continue to infuse me with love for You that originates with You and is worthy of sharing with the world. Amen.

Gary Hewins is the lead pastor of Community Bible Church in the beautiful mountains of Highlands in Western North Carolina. Across the world, people of many nations appreciate Gary's passionate and unique delivery as he rightly divides the word of truth.

With more than twenty-five years of experience as a communicator and consultant, Gary uniquely presents the Word of God in a way that is understandable, challenging, and applicable. His teaching spurs others on to grow in maturity in Christ, discover God's calling on their lives, and impact the world for Him.

Gary holds a Doctor of Ministry degree from Gordon-Conwell Theological Seminary in Boston, Massachusetts. He also serves as the president of Lifepoints Corp., a consulting and training ministry and retreat center for vocational and lay Christian leaders worldwide. Home base for Lifepoints is the tranquil Five Apple Farm in Highlands, North Carolina. (www.FiveAppleFarm.com)

www.ingramcontent.com/pod-product-compliance
Lightning Source LLC
Chambersburg PA
CBHW072024040426

42447CB00009B/1724